Blue
Our hero –
a secret agent

**Chief
Stella Bird**
The SPIES boss

Perch
Chief Stella
Bird's assistant

Professor Z
Invents gadgets
for SPIES

Wing
Astronaut
in charge of
Falcon 8

T0363286

**Commander
Beak**
In charge of the
Pigeon Space
Station

by Debbie White

illustrated by

Rebecca Clements

The Baddies

Birdseed

Super-baddie –
wants to be famous

OXFORD
UNIVERSITY PRESS
AUSTRALIA & NEW ZEALAND

Robo-Dove

Birdseed's giant
robotic dove

OXFORD
UNIVERSITY PRESS

Oxford University Press is a department of the University of Oxford.
It furthers the University's objective of excellence in research, scholarship,
and education by publishing worldwide. Oxford is a registered trademark
of Oxford University Press in the UK and in certain other countries.

Published in Australia by
Oxford University Press
Level 8, 737 Bourke Street, Docklands, Victoria 3008, Australia

Text © Debbie White 2015, 2019

The moral rights of the author have been asserted.

First published 2015
This edition 2019
Reprinted 2020, 2021

ISBN 9780190318239

Series Advisor: Nikki Gamble
Designed by Oxford University Press in collaboration with Miranda Costa
Illustrated by Rebecca Clements
Printed in China by Leo Paper Products Ltd

There are satellites in space, above Earth. Signals from satellites help people to make phone calls and watch TV.

Satellites in action

A TV show from here …

1

… is sent to TVs here …

… here …

… and here.

3

A boy in Singapore phones …

… his Dad in Australia.

At SPIES (the secret spy agency for pigeons), Chief Stella Bird isn't happy.

How many satellites are there above Earth, Agent Blue?

Thousands, Chief!

Well, all the TV satellites have disappeared. No more *Pop Pigeons* until we get them back.

Oh, no!

We need you to go to the Pigeon Space Station and find out what's going on … I suspect Birdseed is up to no good again!

First, Blue tries scuba diving to get an idea of what it feels like to float in space.

Ever been scuba diving before, Blue?

Er, no, Sir!

Next, Blue experiences what take-off will feel like.

Feeling a bit sick, Sir ...

Don't mess up your spacesuit!

Professor Z and Astronaut Wing show Blue the controls on Falcon 8.

Press the Wallaby Warp Drive button to travel super-fast.

Why is it called that?

You travel super-fast, but you bounce like a wallaby.

BOING BOING

Can you guess what the Echidna Defence Shield does?

Does it make Falcon 8 all prickly?

Correct! And the Chameleon Cloaking Device makes Falcon 8 look like ANYTHING you want!

Wing takes Blue to a special training room.

I'm going to show you how to do things while you are weightless.

WEIGHTLESS

First they practise eating while weightless ...

I've never had to chase my beans before!

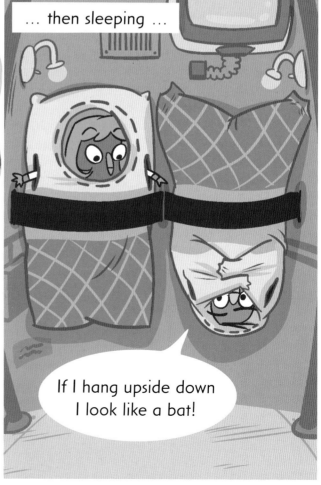

... then sleeping ...

If I hang upside down I look like a bat!

8

... then having a wash ...

No bird baths ... just a washcloth? Can I bring my rubber duck?

... then exercising.

Why do we do two hours of exercise a day?

Being weightless weakens your muscles.

RRRRR!

RRRRRR!

Blue waits nervously to see if he has passed his training.

Well done, Blue. Training complete!

YOU'RE AN ASTRONAUT

The next day, Blue and Wing are waiting for blast-off. Chief calls Blue on the video-phone.

Good luck, Agent Blue. Remember, we need those satellites back!

Yes, Chief!

10 9 8 7 6 5 4 3 2 1

BLAST-OFF!

Blue's stomach flips. The force pins him to his seat and he can't move a feather.

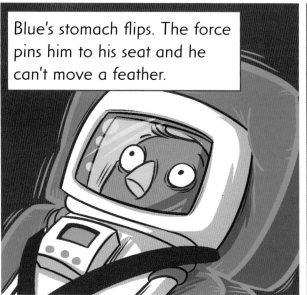

The rocket and shuttle separate.

Coo ... I'm in space!

Wing points out of the shuttle window.

Look!

The Pigeon Space Station! Hooray!

Yes, but what's that thing behind it in the shadows?

As they draw closer, they can see the name 'Swirly Whirly' on the side of the strange shape.

SWIRLY WHIRLY

The Swirly Whirly thing is getting very close to the Pigeon Space Station …

I don't like it, Wing. We have to stop it!

But it's too late. The Space Station is sucked into the swirling hole.

THUNK!

Blue and Wing gasp with horror. Suddenly, a familiar voice booms out over the video-phone …

Super Chef starring ME!
The news … all about ME!
A chat show with ME
interviewing ME!
My name on EVERYTHING.
I'll be **FAMOUS**!

Wing flies Falcon 8 close to the mouth of Swirly Whirly.

I hope this works, Blue.

So do I.
It's going to need split-second timing.

Falcon 8 is sucked inside Swirly Whirly's dark vortex.

SHLURP!

Engage the Echidna Defence Shield. Now!

EEH! OOH! AAH!

THUNK!

HICCUP!

The echidna spikes stick into the sides of Swirly Whirly.
Has the plan worked?

Swirly Whirly detects the blockage.
It engages its reverse suction.

Blue and Wing have everything crossed.

Swirly Whirly's reverse suction is super-powerful. The Echidna Defence Shield struggles to hold them in place.

Later … Swirly Whirly, with Falcon 8 still inside, arrives at the docking bay on Birdseed's Space Base.

We're stopping, Blue. What do we do next?

They turn off the Echidna Defence Shield and set the Chameleon Cloaking Device to 'invisible'.

Blue and Wing jump out of Falcon 8. They creep through Swirly Whirly and into Birdseed's Space Base.

Wow! It's HUGE!

You stay here with Falcon 8, while I search for Birdseed.

But what if Blue doesn't come back? I'm going to follow him.

27

Suddenly, Blue finds himself in a huge control room. He quickly hides, but it's too late.

Agent Blue! What do you think of my Space Base?

Birdseed! How did you know I was here?

The docking bay is fitted with a cloaking-device detector.

Blast! So you knew we were here anyway!

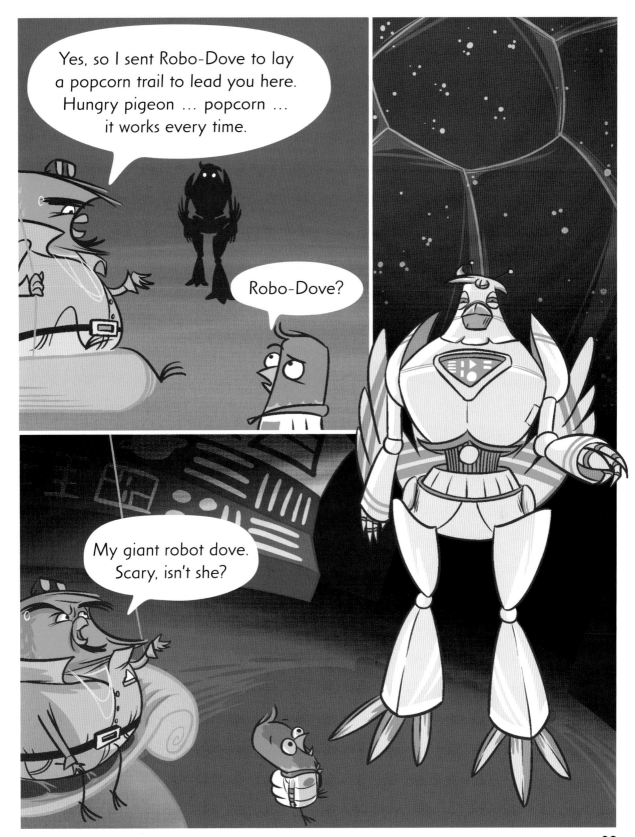

Robo-Dove's eyes light up and she charges at Blue.

Eeek!

Blue turns and flies away, but Robo-Dove is fast. Her beak snaps at Blue's tail.

You can fly, Blue, but you can't hide.

Even in the dark cupboard, Blue can see that Wing is smiling.

On the count of three, they burst out of the cupboard.

Blue distracts Robo-Dove with some interesting dance moves …

Like my funky chicken dance, Robo-Dove?

What about ballet? Do you know *Swan Lake*?

Whoop, whoop … Birdman-style!

… while Wing plucks a feather from her wing.

Robo-Dove is so distracted, she doesn't even notice when Wing flies under her arm.

Tickle, tickle, tickle!

Robo-Dove falls to the floor, laughing.

Hee! Hee! Hee!

As quick as a flash, Blue reaches under Robo-Dove's wing.

CLICK WHIRRR PING!

Birdseed's the enemy. Blue is your friend.

Robo-Dove turns to Blue, smiling.

Horrible Birdseed. Best friend Blue.

Coo … it worked, Wing! But we still need to stop Birdseed.

You think you can stop me, Agent Blue?

Blast! Birdseed's snuck up on us.

Robo-Dove, grab them and bring them to me!

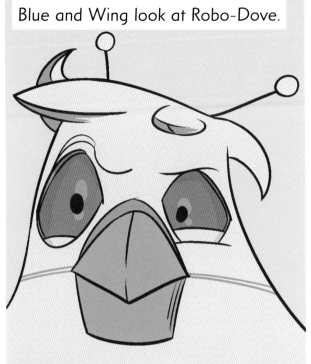

Blue and Wing look at Robo-Dove.

Uh oh. Something's wrong. Robo-Dove should be scaring Blue ... but she's scaring ME!

Big hug, Birdseed.

Birdseed can see the glint in Robo-Dove's eyes. She is planning to give Birdseed a VERY big hug indeed.

Argh ... I'm off! But don't get too comfortable, Agent Blue. I'll be back!

Birdseed turns and runs away. Robo-Dove, Blue and Wing race after him.

They are too slow. Birdseed flies away in his escape pod …
Robo-Dove chases after him.

Birdseed's getting away again!

Never mind. We have his Space Base and Swirly Whirly. We can catch him later.

WHOOMP
WHOOMP
WHOOMP

We need a plan to get the satellites back and working again.

We might even be home in time to watch *Pop Pigeons*!

Robo-Dove shows Blue and Wing how to operate the remote controls for Swirly Whirly. They fly Swirly Whirly back out into space and press the Reverse Suction button.

Look! There's the Pigeon Space Station! Call them to check they're OK.

Agent Blue to Pigeon Space Station … come in Space Station.

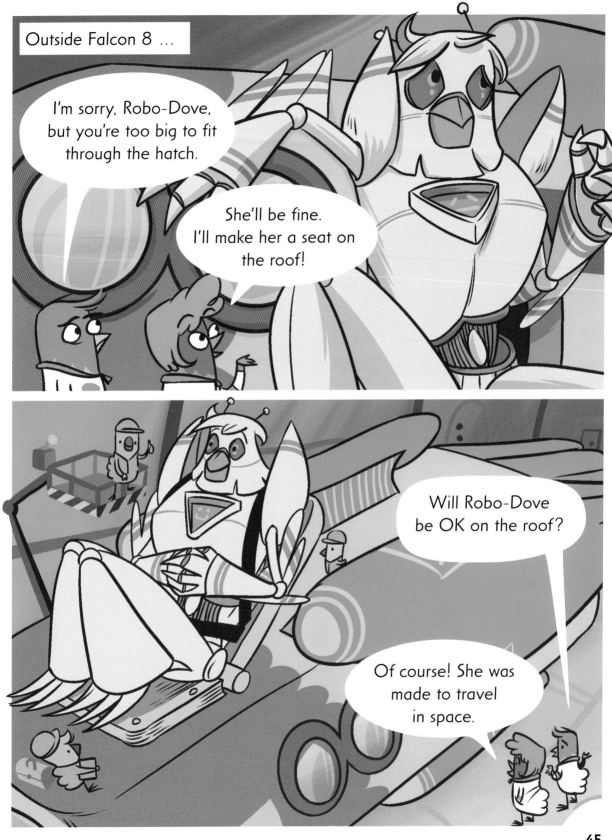

OK, Wing. Let's head home!

BOING BOING BOING

Robo-Dove has a brilliant time. It's like bouncing around on a giant trampoline!

Chief Stella Bird, Perch and Professor Z are waiting when they land.

Well done, Blue and Wing! All the satellites are working again … and I'm pleased to see you've brought … er …

Robo-Dove, Chief. Birdseed stole her from the Pigeon Space Station. Commander Beak said she could come to Earth for a holiday.

Aah … THAT Robo-Dove. Excellent!

To celebrate their safe return, Chief invites everyone to her house for tea and to watch *Pop Pigeons*.

THE END